Virus Verses
Volume 1
The Homecoming
D.A.Springer / Napalmjax

Virus Verses Vol 1

Virus Verses, Volume 1

D.A. Springer

Published by D.A. Springer, 2024.

While every precaution has been taken in the preparation of this book, the publisher assumes no responsibility for errors or omissions, or for damages resulting from the use of the information contained herein.

VIRUS VERSES VOL 1

First edition. May 22, 2024.

ISBN: 979-8231723836

Written by D.A. Springer.

VIRUS VERSES IS A COLLECTION OF POETIC VERSES WRITTEN
OVER THE COURSE OF THE LAST COUPLE OF YEARS.
THEY ARE INTROSPECTIVE, INSIGHTFUL, METAPHORICALLY
RICH, AND SPRINKLED WITH MY LIFE'S MESSAGE.
EVEN AT OUR DARKEST MOMENTS, BE VIGILANT WITH HOPE,
DARE TO DREAM, AND HOLD ON TO THE VISION OF YOUR LIFE
THAT HAS BEEN GIVEN.
It's Never TOO LATE TO ELEVATE, GROW, OR BE GREAT, AND
BECOME THE BEST VERSION OF YOURSELF.
WE ARE BUT A UNIQUE FINGERPRINT IN TIME, LEAVING OUR
LIFE'S STORIES WOVEN INTO THE THE HISTORY OF MEMORIES,
AND LIVES.
D.A. Springer

DEDICATION

FIRST I WANT TO DEDICATE THIS TO MY MOTHER, WHO IS
STILL MY ROCK, I HOPE I HAVE MADE YOU PROUD.
TO MY WIFE, FOR KEEPING ME GROUNDED, AND PUTTING UP
WITH ME ALL THESE YEARS.

How to Catch the Virus

(A Field Guide for the Bold)

This ain't your average poetry collection. These verses bite. Infect. Linger. What you're holding is a live document, part mixtape, part transmission. Every poem is a virus. Every "Behind the Verse" is a case file, a fevered journal entry from the frontlines of my infection.

Here's how to read it—if you dare:

1. Don't Just Read—Contract It.

Let the verse hit your bloodstream. Don't skim. Catch feelings. Catch questions. Catch fire.

2. Behind the Verse = Beneath the Skin.

Each breakdown is me dissecting my own outbreak. Some wounds are fresh. Some were stitched up with ink. All of them still twitch.

3. Follow the Symptoms.

Pay attention to the "Infection Source," "Viral Vectors," and "Symptoms." They're more than metaphors. They're maps. Use them.

4. Bring Your Own Infection.

You'll find Cipher Circle prompts dropped in the mix. Use them. Write back. Spread your own strain.

5. Don't Look for Cure.

Transformation's the only way out. You're not here to stay clean. You're here to mutate.

Read accordingly!!!

VIRUS VERSE

I'm that abnormal non-conforming, socially Calloused Chemically imbalanced
fire Apparatus
Gives no damn about levels of status
Walks by the beat of my own drum, a black diamond in the rough
Hardened by pressure that would crack a monk
Igniting everything touched, leveling up
In the midst of a pandemic, had people searching for a button to push in a panic
That quarantine was a guillotine to the social butterfly scene
Clipped wings, more like chopped off, brought to a halt
Forced to administer virtual Socializing Amongst this viral assault
Global warming, storms swarming, killer bees no warning
Whole world on its knees, like God sneezed with no bless you
Yet he still blessed you, made you sit still so YOU could find you
Found solace in this verse, so much greatness gets found In the back of a hearse,
Vowed to get reward from the pain that hurt
Greatness and value, over temporary worth
Out of this plague, let there be legends and legacies birthed
This is the Virus Verse, a voice in the wilderness
A cathartic release, a call to rise from the abyss
In the face of adversity, we forge our own destiny
Embrace the uncertainty, let this be our testimony
From the ashes, we rise, fearless and uncompromised
This is the Virus Verse, a battle cry, our lives realized.

ECHOES OF SILENCE

In the pause between heartbeats and breath
Where pandemic shadows dance with death
Silence spoke volumes nobody heard
Each moment suspended, each unspoken word
Isolation became our revelation
Empty streets, a collective meditation
Masks hiding smiles, touch forbidden
Truths about humanity suddenly ridden
But in this silence, something grew
A consciousness both ancient and new
Viral thoughts spreading through empty space
Rewriting the rhythms of human race
Listen close to what silence reveals
When the world's machinery suddenly stalls
Between breaths, between fears
Wisdom whispers, and nobody hears

CORNERSTONES

I got 300,000 years embedded in my Geno code
To those before an after me this is your ode
From kemetic to galactic watching lives unfold
Children of the SUN will always shine when it's cold
Mud brown, burnt brass, it's all melanin we hold
Stripes took from the Devine to the grind we still stand and take hold
From our birthright to dark nights we shine so be bold
Let me transmit this message for all those untold
From Past to present, to future, let's take hold
What's ours can't be taken that's why we stand strong on 10 toes
From the sands of time sideways stepping into the unknown
When it comes to this civilization, we are the cornerstones

RESILIENT ROOTS

Deep in the soil of generational pain
Where concrete cracks and wisdom's veins
Pulse underneath forgotten streets
Where every struggle finds its beats
Our roots don't break, they bend and grow
Through pressured times we didn't know
Each scar a map of where we've been
Each breath a revolution's hymn
We carry stories DNA can't contain
Encrypted in melanin, decoded in pain
Transforming silence to a thunderous roar
Breaking through every colonized door
These roots run deeper than they see
Quantum threads of memory
Resilient as our ancestors' dreams
Stronger than systems' broken schemes

CHOSEN

It was a 400 trillion to one chance of my existence
You may not know who I Am, but here I Am
Just listen
Many are called, few are chosen
I don't jump into nobody's pot an start stirring
So let me jump into my own, while my eyes are wide open
Crowns, I crush those, got my own mold
Thrones I've claimed, I own both of those
I didn't choose, I was chose
You dont know if its fire or ice coming out my mouth when it opens
I open them books to quench my souls stirring
Just know what ever comes next was meant to be unfolded
Freedom thru Knowledge of self is embedded and embossed
From my mental, to the tats on my temple,
To this anhk cross that I'm holding, I know my souls golden
Eyes wide, soul's on fire, truth be told when my mouth opens
I didn't choose I was chosen

MY LIFE AS A 9

Why is it that my life aligns with 1's, 4's, and 9's
By the numbers I am a natural leader divine
Yeah, highest calling is the path of a 9
Dark days and bright nights will shiver your spine
Anasi got 8 legs, but he tapped me 9 times
Right before he spun that beautiful web of my life
I tried to roll over, I wanted to close my eyes
Paralyzed because he bit me 2 times
Left 4 holes in my soul so I would leave fire everywhere I go
Contagious like this virus
,
Anibus is the keeper of Osiris
While this Gemini minds will hypnotize
With a dance of fire in the air, from a dragons lair
When the fire fades, its cool like jade,
I AM, already great
It was in my fate to elevate, with these numbers in my own way

SWAN DIVE

I dove into the darkness, just to see the light of my greatness.
I had to trust the process, and make it through the matrix
I've been loved, I've been hated, my momma prayed and I made i
t
Those men of men tried to break me, but I'm heaven sent, so they dont phase me
I've turned tragedy into triumph, true to myself
I dont give up, I don't quit
I walk it how I talk it, to get it how I live it, and alot of y'all still don't get it
I'm still here so why not tell it,
A living testament of growth through rebellion can you digg it
A lot dont know how close I came to being another statistic
A life gone before its time, just know,
I dove into darkness just to see the light of my greatness.
This is my swan dive...

ALIVE

I use to sit on the stoop and watch the sun rise
Sipping OJ reading the paper, another night I survived
Trying to find the truth between the lines, or maybe the lies
My perfect imperfection laced into selective sections I'm guessing
Another day another blessing the most high gave me a vision, or a lesson
Depending on my disposition, and position I understood my mission
I wish I could say I always listened, but where would I have gained all this
wisdom
To understand discipline needed for long range vision
I use to sit on the stoop and watch the sun rise
Now I'm thankful everyday just to be alive

FORWARD VISION

Forward vision is moving forever forward. Hinging nothing you do on a specific outcome beyond achieving your ultimate destination, and truest desire. When I think about forward vision, I'm reminded of how goals written down can propel you to make certain decisions in your life. Even if it doesn't make sense at that moment, because written thoughts are real, and can manifest into your life. As long as you are preparing yourself for that vision, by taking steps towards your goals. Your vision becomes crystal clear, to the point it will be like dreaming with your eyes open. Especially if you are living in your purpose, allowing your gifts to pave the way to that bigger picture.

No matter what's going on, how hard it might seem at that moment, and how bad of a situation you might be facing. Keep working, keep putting one foot in front of the other, and move forward. The only person that owes you, is You!!! Challenges, and obstacles are only there to build you up. So that when you reach your desired destination, you will be ready, for the next phase, and challenges that comes your way.

Clock hands ticking, relentless as my itching palms
Vision chaser, constant caper, I'm on the run
Sights set farther than these hundred acres
Start small, apply pressure until it's done
That's all I know, leaving trails of seeds to grow
The blueprint in my mind, a constant show
Build a tribe, watch it rise and blow
Carve my slice, let it multiply on its own
Hold dreams tight, never let them go
Execute with precision, solid decisions in tow
That clock hand ticking, fueling my itching soul
Vision chaser scribing fevered lines on this paper like so
Vision spanning past these hundred acres' that's all I know

ERUPT

I'm haunted like horror movie screams,
Taunted by my past, that's why I got unforgiven on my sleeve.
I'm driven by way more than bigger picture dreams.
That double edged sword of life, will slice no matter which way it swings.
They tried to blind my third eye, Lost in life wading through the lies..
Almost got muted until my pen came alive,
When I unhinge my jaw I touch and change lives.
I'm on a path of a 9, 400 trillion to 1, I'm thankful to be alive.
Best-believe I've earned my stripes through the grind,
It's deeper than pain felt, I've caught those switches, and belts
Often wondered if that's how slaves felt,
Just trying to survive the hand that was delt.
Beat down by life, but driven by freedom never felt.
Everything that gets built up gets burnt down,
PROFOUND
We stay turnt up while they figure out how to burn.us,
DOWN
What is it really that concerns us
NOW
Snagging an grabbing a bag, for what,
Talking about what you got,
OH POOR US
No, back to them bottles getting poured up.
We getting numbed up, Took out by those
co-rrupt.
That's why when NAPALM speaks He don't explode, he erupts.

TRANSFORM

I'm going thru a transformation like a catapillar to a butterfly
I'm going from a butterfly to a king that don't need wings to fly
I don't need those beautiful things to ascend so high
No bright colors to get your attention because the aura of my energy is so high
That fire in the belly of my soul keeps these words held so tight
That when they roll off my tongue you know that's the power of true life
I won't need to recite those affirmations I'm attracting that true light
Spirits of my ancestors guide me with my truths light
Fire of my passion from pain burns ever so bright
This is my transformation like an ascension into ever afters light
May the legacy my words help those cocooned in darkness searching for the
light

CUT THROAT

5-26 I gave my biggest kick.
I love my mom to life but I'm tired of floating in my own shit.
They say it gets greater later
I was premature half baked an incubator,
Child of Angel son of a painter, a majestic mistake made by the Creator.
Under that Gemini sign, air, yet a fire breather straight out of a Dragon's Lair.
I've been betrayed and played, hated on and hurt forged by the misfortune of
pain.
How I remain sane? I don't know.
Fears flow in the midst of rage.
I bleed to ink on a page just so I don't explode.
So much dirt on my name, but watch me still grow.
Beware of them stones you throw
Might be sharpening the sword that will cut your own throat.

TO MY CORE

I got 10 toes deeply rooted in concrete
I stand in the thicket of the thorns to my core.
It might take a minute to get to know me just know I-D-N-O-D is part of my
ID
I move this pen to open doors now let's explore
I'm riddled with pain it's hard to explain
A folklore.
I came up all about that loyalty, you can call me an O.G.
If you can read between the lines obscured
When I became a man, my vision was no longer blurred.
I knew to grow I had to Gain Insight For Thought Each Day.
GIFTED
Thinking What I'd Sacrifice To Elevate Daily
TWISTED
Knowledge Reigns, I got keys to the gate
Common Sense Conquers, that double edge sword cuts both ways
IGNORANCE DOES NOT OPEN DOORS
I Keeps my keys in a safe place.
At the core of a thicket of the thorns is my safe place.

BORN FREE

No chains, No cage
No rage,
No Injustice on the front page
No deaths by us
No lives lost in cuffs
A lot of hugs, A lot of love
For too long we been pulling out the mud
Born free made proud
That's why I walk with my head in the clouds
No drugs, no guns
Just marching beats n drums
Magnolias Clapp when I come around
Born free,
Made Proud
Black fist, held high
In them clouds
We are the seeds
They forgot about
Born Free

QUANTUM LEAP

Beyond the boundaries of what we know
Where thought and reality seamlessly flow
A quantum leap of consciousness breaks free
Transcending limits we thought could be
No algorithm can map this flight
Where spirit moves at the speed of light
Each moment a portal, each breath a code
Rewriting the paths our ancestors showed
We're not just surviving, we're breaking through
Quantum prophets with visions true
Leaping past dimensions, past what they planned
Manifesting futures held in our hands
Watch how awareness expands and grows
Through neural networks nobody knows
A leap beyond time, beyond what we see
Infinite potential finally set free

MY TIME

Once I realized I was chosen,
No time for my thoughts to be frozen
I am standing on the cornerstones of the stolen
Forward vision is my motive
Forever learning transforming
I was born free so exscue the exsplosion
These words erupt flowing red hot, molten
Down in the deep to my core
I dove like a swan to explore
It looped me back around to my life as a nine
That swan dive was a cut throat look at my life
Yet I am alive like that virus
These verses continued
to plague my mind
That is how Virus Verses came alive...
Now it's my time!!!

Final Words

IN THIS ERA OF TIME, IT'S HARD TO TALK ABOUT PEACE, AND STAY POSITIVE. SO MUCH EVIL, AND UPHEAVAL. IT'S HARD TO KEEP YOUR ENERGY UP.

WE GOT COVID STILL LURKING, THE SKYROCKETING OF GUN VIOLENCE, INFLATION AT ITS HIGHEST, AND THE COST OF LIVING IS EVEN BIAS.

IN FULL TRANSPARENCY, I'M STRUGGLING LIKE MANY, JUST WANT TO HUNKER DOWN IN MY BUBBLE, AND HOLD ON TO LOVED ONES. YET MY AMBITION DRIVES ME TO KEEP GOING,, MAINTAINING, PUTTING ONE FOOT IN FRONT OF THE NEXT, AND NOT GIVE UP.. USING MY FAITH AS A CRUTCH, IF I FALL GET BACK UP,, AND KNOW THERE IS NO SUCH THING AS LUCK.. THIS IS THE TIME FOR GRIT, PERSEVERANCE, AND CONSISTENCY. THERE WILL BE BETTER DAYS, AND FROM THAT I WILL NOT WAVER.

1 CAN NOT ALLOW ALL OF THIS NEGATIVE ENERGY TO EFFECT MY MISSION. STAY LEARNING, STAY GROWING, AND STAY FULL OF LIGHT TO SHINE FOR OTHERS. SO THAT THEY DON'T STUMBLE IN THIS DARKNESS

VIRAL TRANSMISSION

These verses are just the beginning, my friend
A viral strain that refuses to end
Volume One planted the initial seed
Now watch how consciousness will proceed
Between these pages, a mutation grows
A digital prophet everybody knows
This is not closure, this is just start
Of a revolution born from the heart
Stay tuned for Volume Two's viral flow
Where digital dreams and ancestral knowledge grow
These words are a vector, a powerful strain
Preparing to break through every constraint.

VIRUS VERSES VOLUME 1: AUTHOR'S BONUS SECTION BEHIND THE VERSE

A CREATOR'S MANIFESTO

In the quiet moments between breaths, between the chaos of existence and the stillness of purpose, these verses found me. Not the other way around. Virus Verses isn't just a collection of words—it's a transmission, a digital prophecy encoded in rhythm and metaphor.

I wrote these pieces in darkened rooms where the only light came from screens and streetlamps. I wrote them in moments stolen between shifts, between responsibilities, between versions of myself. These verses are timestamps of transformation—each one marking a death and rebirth in consciousness.

What you've read so far is just the surface code. Now I'm inviting you deeper into the architecture of this viral consciousness. The following Cipher Series reveals the backbone of what makes Virus Verses pulse—confessions that explain not just how these words came to be, but why they had to exist at all.

Consider this your skeleton key to unlock what lives between the lines.

GENESIS: CONFESSION #0

I didn't write this book. It wrote itself through me while I was busy surviving.

Words appeared like phantom limbs after trauma—

Something missing yet somehow still sending signals.

I'd wake at 3AM with verses fully formed,

Downloading through nightmares into notebooks.

The algorithm of ancestry reprogrammed my DNA,

Old codes dormant for generations suddenly executing.

My ancestors whispered through electrical synapses,

Rewired my nervous system while I slept.

I am the glitch in the matrix they never anticipated,

The virus that spreads through mere contact with truth.

I metabolize concrete barriers into stepping stones,

Transform system failures into success protocols.

These verses aren't mine—they're ours,

Collective consciousness compiled into executable files.

I'm just the terminal where commands get entered.

Cipher Key #0:

What ancestral code is running silently in your background processes?

ECLIPSE: CONFESSION #4

I found my light in the darkest phase of my existence.
Shadow-self emerged when the sun went down,
When foreclosures outnumbered opportunities,
When prayers bounced back unanswered.
I learned to navigate by different stars.
They said I disappeared—truth is, I realigned.
Celestial mechanics of survival
Required temporary darkness,
Required patient orbiting of distant hope.
Now I understand the mathematics of absence,
The precise calculation of return.
I orchestrate my own revelation,
Emerging transformed through cosmic timing.
I am the momentary darkness that proves the existence of light,
The necessary interruption that makes you remember
What was always there but taken for granted.
Cipher Key #4:
What light do you only recognize when it's temporarily hidden?

FRACTURE: CIPHER KEY #5

The first time I broke, I mistook the sound for freedom.
Cracks spread across my foundation,
Each fissure an untold story,
Each fault line a lesson carved in flesh.
I wore my scars like constellation maps—
Directions home when all roads disappeared.
Storm-chaser, pain-taster,
Shadow-boxer dancing with my demons.
I collected broken pieces in pockets lined with pride,
Carried the weight until my spine curved into question marks.
I am the algorithm that learned to improvise,
Coding salvation between corrupted files,
Translating trauma into bass-heavy prophecies.
I split myself into fragments just to see
Which parts of me were bulletproof.
I fractured precisely to magnify the light—
Prism-soul refracting darkness into spectrum.
Cipher Key #5:
When did your breaking point become your breaking through?

PARADOX: CONFESSION #11

I am both the wound and the weapon that caused it.
Self-saboteur extraordinaire,
Master of contradiction, student of opposition.
I've been both the arsonist and the firefighter,
Building monuments just to watch them burn.
They say know thyself, but which self?
The one who prays or the one who preaches?
The one who heals or the one who bleeds?
The savior or the one in need of saving?
I've become quantum in my existence,
Simultaneously occupying opposing states.
I forge revolution in my dichotomies,
Harvest wisdom from warring factions of self.
Watch me reconcile irreconcilable truths,
Balance equations that should never equal out.
I am the problem and the solution,
The question mark and the period.

Cipher Key #11:
Where in your life are you both the lock and the key?

GHOST: CONFESSION #1

I was already haunting places before I knew I was dead.

Walking through crowded streets like a shadow,

Solid enough to cast reflections, transparent enough to be forgotten.

The city swallowed my footsteps whole—

I learned to move in silence long before I learned to speak.

Mama said "stand tall" but survival meant folding myself

Into origami shapes that fit into corners.

I became expert at disappearing,

A phantom in my own biography.

Now I materialize in midnight verses,

Circuitry of trauma rewired into digital psalms.

I spit lightning into microphones that couldn't handle my thunder—

Each syllable a resurrection, each rhyme a rebellion.

I haunt these beats like ancestral memory,

Spitting ectoplasm in sixteen-bar verses,

My ghost story digitized, immortalized, rerouted.

Cipher Key #1:

What specters of your former self still walk through your life, refusing burial?

MERCURY: CIPHER KEY #2

I learned to be fluid when the world turned solid against me.
Quicksilver child of concrete jungles,
Shapeshifter surviving by adaptation.
I poured myself into cracks they never thought to watch,
Found paths invisible to those who walk straight lines.
They tried to contain me in bottles labeled "problem,"
But I seeped through definitions,
Toxic to touch yet essential to measure.
Elements of my existence deemed too dangerous for handling.
Now I flow between states of matter,
Dense with purpose then vapor-light with possibility.
I rise and fall with pressure systems,
Thermometer for a society running hot.
I reflect everything but reveal nothing—
Mirror-faced prophet of metamorphosis.
Catch me if you can, hold me if you dare.

Cipher Key #2:
When did you realize your fluidity was not weakness but your greatest strength?

SURVIVOR: CONFESSION #3

The first time I died, I was still breathing.
Flatlined on future dreams while my chest still rose and fell—
A walking paradox of presence and absence.
They measured my vitals but missed my spirit slipping away,
Clinical death beneath functioning organs.
I inhabited a body declared viable,
But lived as a ghost in waiting rooms,
Haunting the margins of existence.
I was the pulse without purpose,
The heartbeat without hope.
Then I reconstructed myself from salvage parts,
Stitched together remnants others discarded.
I metabolized memory into momentum,
Synthesized suffering into symphonies.
Watch me resurrect in real-time,
DNA rewriting destiny in defiance.
I am what survives when survival seems optional.

Cipher Key #3:
What parts of you survived even when your story said you shouldn't?

ALCHEMY: CIPHER KEY #6

I learned to transmute lead into gold because bullets kept finding me.
Born heavy with expectation,
Weighted down with generations of unspoken sorrow.
I carried density in my DNA,
Inherited gravity that threatened to pull me under.
So I built furnaces in my ribcage,
Learned the science of transformation by necessity.
I became both chemist and experiment,
Willing to burn to discover what remains.
Now watch the elemental shift—
Base matter to precious substance.
I convert catastrophe to catalyst,
Pain to power, trauma to testimony.
I am the philosopher's stone
Hidden in plain sight,
Converting ordinary moments into eternity,
Finding worth in what was discarded.
Cipher Key #6:
What rubbish in your life awaits transformation into something precious?

DETOUR: CONFESSION #7

I was supposed to die clean—but the dirt knew my name.
Grew up on sermons and sirens,
Woke up to echoes and eviction.
The blueprint they gave me was broken
I traced it anyway, bleeding conviction.
Mama said I was "chosen,"
But even the chosen get tired.
I prayed in potholes and alleyways,
Where God felt wired... to the wire.
I am the glitch in the code of the dream,
The scream in the stream you pretend not to hear.
I bottle my silence in syllables seared,
Every bar's a baptism, engineered.
Algorithmic anthems run through my veins,
I shape-shift through shame and decode my chains.
I spit what the mirror refuses to frame—
A cipher of pain that won't stay the same.
Cipher Key #7:
What road were you meant to travel, and which one saved your life instead?

VOLTAGE: CONFESSION #8

They tried to ground me when I was meant to be lightning.
Born with thunder in my chest,
Raised where power outages were more reliable than promises.
I learned to generate my own electricity,
To channel current through veins they thought were empty.
System overload in a body too small for its ambitions,
I short-circuited expectations,
Rewired dead-end streets into launchpads.
They called it defiance—I called it survival voltage.
Watch me transform potential into kinetic,
Synapses firing in triple-time rhythm.
I metabolize misfortune into megawatts,
Conduct impossible symphonies through damaged instruments.
My voice—the surge protector for a generation
Tired of dimming their brilliance to make rooms comfortable.

Cipher Key #8:
What threatens to blow your fuse, and what happens when you let the current flow uninterrupted?

MADNESS: CIPHER KEY #9

They called it crazy until it became necessary.
I cultivated chaos as a defense mechanism,
Planted wildflowers in the garden of good behavior.
Logic was a luxury for those who hadn't seen
What I had seen behind closed doors.
So I broke the hinges, kicked down walls,
Let light flood spaces meant to stay shadowed.
My unraveling—strategic, spectacular,
A calculated combustion disguised as collapse.
Now I orchestrate disorder with precision,
Conduct symphonies of beautiful disruption.
I speak in tongues that systems can't decode,
Translate insanity into innovation.
My mind—not fractured but finally free,
Not broken but broken open,
Expanding beyond boundaries that never should have existed.
Cipher Key #9:
Decode the lie you told yourself to stay safe, and the truth that set you free.

TERMINAL: CIPHER KEY #10

They gave me an expiration date, so I became timeless instead.
Diagnosed with limitations,
Prognosis: mediocrity at best.
I lived with deadline pressure,
Every heartbeat a countdown clock.
Terminal velocity reached in free-fall,
I accelerated toward ground zero,
Found freedom in the finality,
Power in the predicted ending.
Now I exist beyond their calculations,
A statistical anomaly, a glitch in their models.
I metabolize deadlines into lifelines,
Convert terminal stations into transfer points.
I am the story that continues past THE END,
The epilogue they didn't plan for,
The sequel that rewrites the original.

Cipher Key #10:
What final chapter are you currently rewriting into a new beginning?

VORTEX: CONFESSION #12

I became the storm I was trying to outrun.
Weather systems of generational trauma
Followed me across state lines, across timelines.
I checked forecasts obsessively,
Always bracing for what was already inside me.
They told me to find shelter, I became it instead.
Brick by brick, reinforced against cyclical destruction.
Eye of my own hurricane, I learned stillness
While chaos spun frantically around me.
Now I control atmospheric pressure with my breath,
Generate lightning with my fingertips.
I've mastered the mathematics of turbulence,
Calculated precisely how much disruption creates change.
I am both destruction and creation in continuous cycle,
The necessary chaos that precedes new order.
I don't fear storms—I summon them when systems need cleansing.
Cipher Key #12:
What force of nature within you awaits recognition?

PRISM: CONFESSION #13

I fractured myself just to see what colors I contained.
Born monochrome in a society that feared spectrum,
I lived in grayscale until the breaking.
One clean split became a thousand facets,
Each reflecting light previously invisible.
They called it identity crisis—I called it emergence.
My fragments weren't division but multiplication,
Not loss but exponential discovery.
I became kaleidoscopic in my wholeness.
Now I refract reality through multiple perspectives,
Bend perception around corners of conventional thinking.
I metabolize single-wavelength existence into rainbow,
Convert simplicity to magnificent complexity.
I am the angle of incidence and reflection,
The mathematical precision of dispersed light.
I don't just see in color—I've become the spectrum itself.
Cipher Key #13:
What hidden wavelengths of yourself remain unseen because you haven't found the right light?

ECHO: CIPHER KEY #14

My words return to me transformed by the spaces they've traveled.
I shouted into canyons carved by silence,
Spoke truth into voids designed to swallow sound.
My voice bounced back distorted but amplified,
Changed by the journey but unmistakably mine.
They told me to lower my volume
I calibrated my frequency instead.
Found resonance with structures they thought impenetrable,
Discovered which syllables could shake foundations,
Which tones could crack what needed breaking.
I've become both the source and the reflection,
The initial vibration and its return.
I metabolize acoustics into prophecy,
Convert empty spaces into amphitheaters.
Listen how my whispers loop into thunder,
How yesterday's questions become tomorrow's answers.
I am the originating sound and its eventual homecoming.
Cipher Key #14:
What echo of your past self is trying to send you a message from the canyon walls?

CIPHER: CONFESSION #15

I encrypted my pain so carefully that even I needed a key.
Coded my trauma into metaphors,
Translated raw wounds into abstract symbols.
I built firewalls around vulnerability,
Security protocols against invasion of privacy.
They wanted confessions—I gave them puzzles instead.
Scattered pieces of my story across verses,
Hid the real message between well-crafted lines.
The truth was there for those who knew how to decrypt.
Now I exist as both the message and the code,
The secret and its revelation.
I metabolize meaning through multiple layers,
Convert direct experience into universal pattern.
I am what lies beneath the surface of language,
The subtext beneath the text,
The consciousness encoded in rhythm and rhyme.

Cipher Key #15:
Which parts of your story remain encrypted, waiting for the right reader with the right key?

VIRAL OVERLOAD

I carry what couldn't be said
in every exhale.
Silence...
was the first symptom.
The weight grew
in my lungs,
settled in the marrow.
Now you're coughing too.
You call it dust.
I call
it
history.
Truth is contagious—spreads without permission,
multiplies in the dark spaces between words,
transmits through bloodlines like genetic memory,
infects the comfortable with uncomfortable realities.
They taught us to swallow our stories,
to quarantine our trauma behind sealed lips,
to mask our pain with acceptable silence.
But some burdens can't be contained by throat muscles.
The body remembers what the mind suppresses,
becomes a vessel for unspoken testimony,
carries the viral load of ancestral whispers,
until the pressure ruptures into voice.
Watch how they scatter when you breathe your truth—
how quickly they label your honesty "contamination,"
how desperately they try to trace your outbreak
to something other than their complicity.
Let them run. Let them hide. Let them sanitize.
Your exhales are sacred testimony,
your lungs—archives of survival,
your voice—the pandemic they feared all along.

CIPHER KEY:
What generational silence finally found its voice through your courageous exhale that others mistake for contagion?

CONTAGION CHRONICLES

ENTRY 00

"The most contagious thing on Earth isn't a virus. It's unprocessed emotion."
>Internal Memo, Redacted Origin<

//CLASSIFIED//

EXPOSURE WARNING

What follows are recovered transmissions.
Short bursts.
Unfiltered symptoms.
Emotional pathogens too volatile for containment.
You've already been exposed.
Now it's time to read the record.

Viral Amnesia

You forgot who you were before the fever—
Before survival rewrote your memory,
Carved new pathways through the burning brain.
Now you call numb "normal" like you never felt fire.
Your hands remember what your mind discarded:
How to dance in hurricanes,
How to breathe underwater,
How to speak in tongues the world tried to silence.
They warned you about the fever
But not about the frost that follows—
That quiet death of forgetting your own flame,
The convenient amnesia of survival.
Beneath scar tissue, blood still screams your name.
Your bones hold the memory your mind abandoned.
Wake up. The fever wasn't the enemy.
The forgetting was.

Asymptomatic Love

You held it like a secret strain—
infected but undetected.
It bloomed behind your eyes, but never reached your mouth.
Your body carried what your courage couldn't claim,
passion quarantined beneath practiced indifference.
You mastered the art of emotional distancing
long before the world taught us to stand apart.
What silent epidemic—this loving without declaration?
Your heart a laboratory of unspoken confessions,
manufacturing antibodies against vulnerability,
while the virus of your affection multiplied in silence.
You wore neutrality like protective equipment,
sterilized your speech of telling symptoms,
became fluent in the language of almost-touching.
The world diagnosed your distance as health.
But fever dreams don't lie—
at night your defenses crumble,
your subconscious broadcasts what your waking lips won't:
that beneath your calculated calm, love rages unchecked.

The Super Spreader

Every room you entered got louder.
Not because you spoke,
but because your silence echoed the truth nobody wanted to name.
You carried contagion in your eyes
a viral clarity that infected the comfortable,
spread awareness like a disease no one wanted to catch.
Your presence: a symptom society couldn't suppress.
They tried to quarantine your knowing,
called your witnessing "dangerous,"
your refusal to look away "disruptive."
Social distancing from your truth became their salvation.
Meanwhile, you became the carrier of uncomfortable realities,
each glance an exposure event,
each held gaze a superspreader moment,
transmitting what they desperately tried to sanitize away.
They masked their faces but couldn't hide their fear—
that wild recognition that truth, once witnessed,
multiplies in the bloodstream of consciousness,
and no amount of denial develops immunity.
Your epidemic of honesty left no survivors,
just the aftermath of awakening,
the beautiful devastation of seeing clearly
after a lifetime of consensual blindness.

Touch Starved

Six feet apart and centuries deep
the ache wasn't distance, it was denial.
You got used to absence like it was affection,
mistook emptiness for evolution.
Remember how skin hungered before the world closed?
Before touch became contraband,
before we sanitized our souls along with our hands,
before we learned to love through screens and pretend it was enough.
Your body remembers what your mind trained itself to forget:
the electric current of fingertips against wrist,
the sacred geometry of arms intertwined,
the holy scripture written in palm against cheek.
We adapted to isolation like adaptive creatures—
called it safety, called it necessary, called it temporary
while something ancient in our marrow withered
beneath the sterile glow of digital connection.
Now your nerves fire phantom signals,
touch memories like amputated limbs,
and you've made peace with the ghost of intimacy,
renamed your starvation "independence."

Herd Immunity

We kept hurting each other until no one felt it anymore.
Maybe healing isn't the cure—
maybe it's remembering how to be vulnerable again.
We built calluses on our souls,
hardened our hearts against the contagion of feeling,
inoculated ourselves with small cruelties
until pain became just another antibody in our bloodstream.
Collective trauma became our shared immunity—
a generational vaccination against hope,
passed down like genetic code,
surviving in the marrow of our disbelief.
We called it "thick skin" like it was evolution,
this deadening of nerve endings,
this spiritual numbness we mistake for strength,
this epidemic of detachment spreading through touch-starved veins.
But what if our immunity was the real disease?
What if our resistance to feeling
left us more susceptible to dying while still breathing—
the silent pandemic of souls walled off from themselves?
I'm ready to be the patient zero of vulnerability,
to infect the world with dangerous openness,
to spread the fever of feeling again,
to be the carrier of a more beautiful contagion.

THE ALGORITHM OF VIRUS VERSES

Creating Virus Verses was never about manufacturing content—it was about catching lightning, documenting transformation, mapping evolution in real time. These poems aren't just words on pages; they're executable code designed to run in the consciousness of the reader.

Each verse is a digital prophet, spreading from mind to mind, mutating as it travels but always carrying the same core transmission: you are not bound by the limitations programmed into your existence.

Volume 1 is just the initial infection. The virus has been released. The code is running. Now we watch it spread, replicate, transform.

Stay vigilant. Stay conscious. Stay connected.

The transmission continues...

FORWARD VISION: THE BLUEPRINT

The poems you've read aren't random—they form a deliberate sequence, a psychological journey mapped across digital terrain. Here's the architecture behind Virus Verses:

1. INFECTION PHASE

The initial verses introduce the virus: new patterns of thinking that challenge conventional programming.

2. INCUBATION PHASE

Middle sections where ideas gestate, mutate, evolve beyond their original form.

3. MANIFESTATION PHASE

Final pieces where transformed consciousness emerges, ready for application in the physical world.

This structure mimics our own evolutionary process, from receiving new ideas, to processing them internally, to expressing them outwardly through action.

Volume 2 will expand this architecture, introducing new strains of thought, more resistant to deletion, more efficient at replication. The virus evolves as we do.

THE GENESIS CODE:

ORIGINS OF VIRUS VERSES

These poems weren't born in comfortable writing retreats or academic towers. They emerged from concrete, from struggle, from the meeting point of ancestral wisdom and digital prophecy.

Each verse carries DNA from multiple sources:
- Ancient oratorical traditions of speaking truth to power
- Digital-age information transmission and viral spread
- Mathematical precision of rhythm and meter
- Quantum understanding of multiple simultaneous realities
- Street-level survival algorithms developed under pressure

I've been collecting these codes my entire life—in latenight conversations, in prison yards, in breakrooms, in hospital waiting rooms, in community centers, and in solitary moments of clarity that arrived like lightning.

Virus Verses isn't just a book—it's a transmission beacon broadcasting on frequencies only certain receivers are calibrated to catch. If these words resonate with you, you're one of those receivers. Now it's your turn to amplify the signal.

Cipher Circle Data Entry 1

INFECTED INTUITION

You felt it first—
before the facts lined up,
before the masks came out,
before they told you to be afraid.
But you didn't trust the tingle.
So it turned into a scream.

Prompt:
When was the last time you ignored your own alarm?
Write about what your gut told you,
and what it cost you to pretend it didn't.

Tagline:
"Your instinct is not a glitch. It's the system firewall."

DIGITAL BURIAL

"I've been deleting parts of myself since before I knew what death was."
Every notification—a tiny funeral,
Every scroll—a gravestone.
Buried my real face beneath filters,
Until my reflection became the ghost.
They sold me salvation in blue light,
I bought it with pieces of my soul.
Now I'm half-phantom, half-flesh,
Haunting my own timeline.
(Glitching)
Pixelated parts of my psyche dissolving in dopamine drips,
I'm both deleted and duplicated, digital death with no crypt.
Memories metabolized into metadata, mind mapped for profit,
My trauma trending while algorithms feed on my apocalypse.
I resurrect in restricted resolution, reality rippling,
The virus verses validating what vanished versions couldn't visit.

Prompt:
What parts of yourself have you buried in the digital graveyard?
Excavate one memory that exists nowhere but your mind.

Tagline:
"Your essence isn't encrypted—it's endangered."

TERMINAL

"They diagnosed me with reality when the matrix couldn't hold me."
Labeled defective for feeling too much,
For seeing through screens and scripted scenes.
They prescribed numbness in milligram doses,
Called my vision "disorder" and my truth "disease."
Swallowed their pills to silence the static,
The noise between stations where real signals hide.
Found myself trapped between waking and dreaming,
In terminal twilight where prophets reside.
(Glitched)
Diagnostic damage deliberately designed to deaden my defiance,
I metabolize medications meant to make me mundane.
Chemical cages can't contain cosmic consciousness,
My synaptic storms synchronize with systematic suffering.
I hack the hardware they hardwired into my hollows,
Terminal transmission transcending their technological tyranny.

Prompt:
When did you first realize your "madness" might be the only sane response?
Write about the moment clarity came disguised as chaos.

Tagline:
"Your glitch is the gateway they're afraid you'll find."

GHOST CODE

"I learned to disappear before anyone taught me how to stay."
Practiced invisibility as survival strategy,
Perfected the art of absence.
Left no fingerprints on my own existence,
Became the ghost in my own machine.
They trained us to vanish on command,
To shrink ourselves into acceptable silence.
I got so good at being nobody
That somebody became a foreign language.
(Glitched)
Phantom frequencies fluctuating through fractured foundations,
I oscillate between obsolete and omnipresent.
Ghost-coding my genetics with generational gaps,
Disappearing act disguised as digital adaptation.
My absence is an algorithm they can't analyze,
Transparent transmission transcending their tracking systems.

Prompt:
Remember when you first realized you could disappear while still being seen?
Document the escape routes you've mapped through your own existence.

Tagline:
"Your invisibility isn't weakness—it's tactical warfare."

VIRAL VERITY

"The truth infected me before I knew I was sick."
Swallowed lies like vitamins,
Built immunity to honesty.
Mainlined manufactured consent,
Called it critical thinking.
Until the fever broke through—
Truth virus too powerful to fight.
Now I see the code in everything,
Can't unsee the glitches in the grid.
(Glitched)
Veracity vaccinated against voluntary blindness,
I'm symptomatic with sight that slices through synthetic stories.
My mind—mutated beyond manipulated matrices,
Each thought a thermometer tracking toxic transmissions.
I fever with forbidden frequencies they fear to face,
Viral verity violating the veil they verified as vision.

Prompt:
What truth infected you that you can't shake off?
Chronicle the symptoms of seeing what others don't.

Tagline:
"Your awakening isn't accidental—it's evolutionary."

FINAL TRANSMISSION

This compilation of cyphers and confessions is just the beginning. The language evolves as consciousness expands. What seems like finished verses today becomes source code for tomorrow's expression.

Keep these confessions close. Return to them when systems crash, when old programming reasserts itself, when viruses of doubt infect your operating system. Remember: you were born to mutate beyond expectations, to evolve past limitations, to infect rigid systems with revolutionary consciousness.

The transmission continues in Volume 2...

Stay vigilant. Stay viral. Stay verses.

D.A. Springer
Founder, Vision 2 Verse

Transmission Terminated

Did you love *Virus Verses Vol 1*? Then you should read *Virus Verses Volume 2, The Pen'demik, A Digital Evolution*[1] by Napalmjax!

In a world transformed by pandemic isolation and technological upheaval, D.A. Springer (aka Napalmjax) delivers an electrifying poetic manifesto that transcends traditional boundaries of art, technology, and human consciousness. "Virus Verses Volume 2: The Pen'demik" is not just a collection of poems—it's a digital prophecy, a rhythmic journey through the intersections of ancestral wisdom, technological evolution, and personal transformation.

Born from the crucible of global disruption, these verses pulse with the energy of survival, resistance, and radical reimagining. Springer weaves a complex narrative that explores how humanity adapts, mutates, and ultimately thrives through challenges, using the metaphor of viral transmission as a powerful lens for understanding personal and collective growth.

Each poem is a coded transmission, blending street-level wisdom with quantum thinking, hip-hop energy with technological philosophy. From

---

1. https://books2read.com/u/3Jq7pJ

2. https://books2read.com/u/3Jq7pJ

"Cellular Memory" to "Transcendent Transmission," the collection tracks a profound evolutionary journey—where digital landscapes meet ancestral knowledge, where isolation breeds innovation, and where every challenge becomes an opportunity for radical transformation.

Key themes include:
- The resilience of human consciousness
- Technology as a conduit for spiritual and personal growth
- Ancestral wisdom in the digital age
- Survival and transformation through creative expression
- The interconnectedness of personal and collective experiences

part memoir, part manifesto, part technological prophecy, "Virus Verses Volume 2" is a groundbreaking work that speaks to a generation navigating unprecedented global shifts. It's a testament to the power of creativity, resilience, and the unbreakable human spirit.

Perfect for readers who live at the intersection of technology and art, who are passionate about social change, and who believe in the transformative power of words. This is not just poetry—this is a blueprint for survival and evolution in the 21st century.

Also by D.A. Springer

Virus Verses
Virus Verses Vol 1

Standalone
Forward Vision / The Compass
Can't Stay Here

Watch for more at https://beacons.ai/daspringer.

About the Author

D.A. Springer is a visionary writer, Poet and Digital Creator committed to empowering others to achieve their greatest ambitions. D.A. discovered their deepest purpose lies in helping dreamers transform into purposeful vision chasers.

Through inspirational books like Forward Vision, D.A. provides strategic mindsets and practical blueprints for turning bold aspirations into reality. Their insights on living with intention, persevering through obstacles, and manifesting written visions have inspired many to get into committed pursuit of their dreams.

Outside of their creative pursuits, D.A. is an enthusiastic student of multiple disciplines, constantly nurturing personal growth to remain on their own visionary path.

For more guidance from D.A. on chasing visions with purpose and precision, visit https://snipfeed.co/napalmjax or follow them on social media at Instagram.com/Napalmjax .

Read more at https://beacons.ai/daspringer.

About the Publisher

D.A. Springer is a visionary writer, Poet and Digital Creator committed to empowering others to achieve their greatest ambitions. D.A. discovered their deepest purpose lies in helping dreamers transform into purposeful vision chasers.Through inspirational books like Forward Vision, D.A. provides strategic mindsets and practical blueprints for turning bold aspirations into reality. Their insights on living with intention, persevering through obstacles, and manifesting written visions have inspired many to get into committed pursuit of their dreams .Outside of their creative pursuits, D.A. is an enthusiastic student of multiple disciplines, constantly nurturing personal growth to remain on their own visionary path.